OSHÚN

SANTERÍA AND THE ORISHA OF LOVE, RIVERS & SENSUALITY

BY BABA RAUL CANIZARES

ORIGINAL PUBLICATIONS
PLAINVIEW, NEW YORK

Oshún

Santería and the Orisha of Love, Rivers & Sensuality

by Baba Raul Canizares

© ORIGINAL PUBLICATIONS 2001

ISBN: 0-942272-69-2

All rights reserved. No part of this book may be reproduced in any manner whatsoever, including Internet usage, without written permission from Original Publications, except in the case of brief quotations embodied in critical articles and reviews.

Please be advised that we cannot make any claims of supernatural effects or powers for any of the formulas, spells, rituals, etc. listed herein. The Author offers the contents for interest, folklore value, experimentation and whatever value it may have to the reader thereof. This book is offered as a Literary Curio Only. No responsibility whatsoever for the contents or the validity of the statements herein is assumed by the author, publisher or seller of this book.

FIRST EDITION
First Printing 2001

Artwork by Raul Canizares

Original Publications
P.O. Box 236
Old Bethpage, New York 11804-0236
(516) 454-6809

Printed in the United States of America

INTRODUCTION

Her eyes sparkle in the forest,
her eyes sparkle in the river.
She is the wisdom of the forest,
she is the wisdom of the river. [1]

In the Cuban context, all deities are imported. The island's native population was decimated long ago, their gods leaving our soil with the souls of the Siboney, the Taino, the Guanacabibe and the Carib who couldn't take the barbarous abuse the Spaniards gave out under the aegis of a dying god. After the demise of the native population, the fertile land called Cubanacan, meaning "mainland," lost its connection to the people who inhabited it. That connection which only indigenous folk can have with the earth was re-established when the Spaniards began to import African slaves. Unwittingly, the Spaniards had given to Cuba that which it had lost, an indigenous population, and a people who understood the language of nature. The Africans became the de-facto native population of Cuba.

When Christopher Columbus first saw the island of Cuba he stated "this is the most beautiful land human eyes have ever seen." With its lush vegetation, beaches featuring pristine white sands, and lovely mountains, the island of Cuba indeed possesses breathtaking beauty. First peopled by four different native American groups (the Taino, the Siboney, the Guanacabibe and the ferocious Carib), the land was later colonized by the Spaniards, themselves a multi-ethnic, multi-cultural, and multi-lingual group. It was the Spaniards who imported African slaves of several different ethnicities to replace the decimated native population, making Cuba a true melting pot of cultures, nations, and ethnicities.

Columbus tried to name the island "Juana," in honor of a Spanish princess; of the three Spanish islands in the Caribbean, only Cuba, for reasons I don't know, rejected its "Catholic" name. Perhaps this was an omen of how the Cuban ethos would develop, where Catholic priests had to be imported because the populace was not interested in serving the Church at that level. In fact, most Cubans would say *"yo soy Catolico a mi manera,"* meaning *"I'm a Catholic in my own way."* This usually meant that, with the possible exception of the ban against murder, all commandments were there to be broken. *"Catolico a mi manera"* also became a euphemism, a password, for people who while covering their exterior with the respectability of Catholicism, in fact worshipped the gods of the slaves.

Cuba became a true socio-cultural melting pot. Cuba's idea of the perfect woman was also influenced by this melting pot milieu, where the image that emerged was a stereotypical *"bella mulata",* the gorgeous mixed-race, bronze-skinned, wavy-haired siren possessing luscious, full lips, shiny caramel-colored eyes, firm, not-too-large breasts, a tiny waist and a prodigious butt held by thick, well-formed thighs and ample hips. This peculiarly Cuban idea of female beauty, which even other Latinos thought somewhat over-the-top, was thought to be embodied by the goddess Oshún, who, although she had been black in Africa, was magically transformed into La Bella Mulata.

The Santería goddess Oshún is in many ways different from her African counterpart. The Yorubaland orisha is goddess of only one river, the one that bears her name, and is mainly known as one of Shangó's three wives. In Cuba she has been apotheosized as the Divine Epitome of female sensuality, the owner of all rivers, and the one who rules over gold and copper. Her popularity in Cuba is total and unsurpassed by any other orisha; she is Cuba's patron saint, the beloved symbol of Cuban womanhood. Oshún's more subtle characteristics are embodied in her Catholic counterpart, the beloved image of Our Lady known as *"Nuestra*

"La Bella Mulata"

Señora de La Caridad del Cobre" (Our Lady of Charity from the Township of Cobre). The township of Cobre, in Cuba's easternmost province, Oriente, is situated near copper mines, thus the name *"Cobre,"* which means, "Copper." The image is that of a copper-skinned, long-haired young Madonna appearing to three men in a rowboat, one white, one black, and one Indian, symbolizing her patronage over all Cubans, regardless of their race. Cubans call their Virgin simply *"Caridad"* or *"Cachita,"* its nickname. Cuba's love affair with Oshún /Cachita is an ongoing one, now also being shared by millions of others who come to know the Caribbean character of the West African goddess Oshún.

In one of her avatars, Oshún Panchagara, she is depicted as a Holy Whore, *"La Santa Puta".* This is a controversial aspect of the orisha, rejected as a New World fabrication by modern-day Yoruba revisionists and African American feminists who feel their goddess is being degraded by depictions of her as a prostitute. These people are actually projecting their own prejudices and morality into the equation. In reality, prostitution has not always been viewed as degrading or immoral. In fact, temple prostitutes, including the famous "vestal virgins" of ancient Rome, have featured prominently in the history of ancient religions. On and off, prostitution has been legal in Cuba until the late 1960's. It is only natural that, just as every other profession has a patron saint, prostitutes also enjoy this privilege. In her aspect as Panchagara, Oshún is at her most rambunctious, coquettish, and wild. Panchagara is La Bella Mulata on Steroids, a woman very much in control who chooses who she'll bless with her sexual favors. Panchagara is in no way a victim, as those who object to her claim, but an empowered female who has chosen prostitution on her terms and for her gain. Oshún Panchagara has been an inspiration to women who for whatever reason have had to engage in prostitution; she demonstrates that a human being's sense of self-worth need not be affected by what he or she does for a living.

Oshún Panchagara
"La Santa Puta"

1

Pataki!
SACRED STORIES ABOUT OSHÚN

Oshún brings Ogun back to civilization

There was a time when Ogun, the god of Iron, was banned from
Orishaland after falling out of favor with his father, Obatala. Ogun then
decided to move deep into the jungle where no man or orisha could find
him. Unfortunately, Ogun had not completed the process of transferring
his knowledge of how to work with iron to humankind at large. Shortly
after Ogun left, the whole community of gods and men began to be impacted
by the absence of well-made iron implements. When word of these
happenings reached Obatala, the king of all Orisha, he decreed that Ogun,
although still banned from Orishaland, was to resume his position as master
blacksmith at the other end of the country in a place called Nupe, where
Ogun had once lived with Oya. No one, however, could convince Ogun
to return. Finally, Oshún offered to lure Ogun back to civilization with her
magic honey. Oshún, most beauteous of females, ruler of all rivers,
Obatala's favorite, was the most irresistible of women, surely Ogun would
follow the sweet smell of Oshún's honey. Spreading honey on her
curvaceous form, the naked beauty set out for the jungle. Ogun's keen
sense of smell was overwhelmed with the sweet-sour delight of Oshún's
honey. Almost in a trance, the muscular, bearded man appeared next to
Oshún. She put her fingers, drenched in honey, inside Ogun's mouth, he
could not resist following Oshún, trying to embrace her. Oshún always

managed to slip off Ogun's embrace, forcing the mesmerized titan to follow her back to civilization. Once there, messengers from Obatala told Ogun he was to remain in Nupe, teaching others the art of the blacksmith. Ogun, ever the dutiful son in spite of his past sins, obeyed. It was in this way that Oshún brought iron-making back to humankind.

Commentary: Oshún's honey is an allegory for female love-making. It was using female guile, not brute force, that Oshún was able to convince the irascible god of the forge to bring back to civilization the indispensable gift of knowing how to make iron tools and weapons.

Oshún gives Shangó a taste of her honey.

Oshún and Shangó

His three sisters, Dada, Yemayá, and Oshún had raised Shangó. Of these, Oshún was the youngest. Although at this stage of world history brother-sister marriage was not considered incestuous, the fact that Oshún had helped raise Shangó made it shameful for her to make her sexual attraction to him known. She, as the embodiment of female sexuality, was naturally attracted to her male counterpart, Shangó. After Shangó married his other sisters Oba and Oya, Oshún's passion for him knew no bounds. One day, she decided to consummate her desire. Wearing nothing but her honey, she emerged from her golden river as Shangó was washing himself. With the sphere of the sun behind her svelte, perfect shape, Oshún seemed to be the epitome of what beauty in a woman should be. Forgetting the motherly respect he had been taught to feel for Oshún, he fell on her like a bull in heat, possessing her over and over, reaching a total of sixty-six orgasms one after the other in a period of sixteen days, during which time neither slept, ate, or did anything but copulate.

A palace guard interrupted the fiery lovers. Obatala wanted to see both immediately. Facing their irate father, Shangó and Oshún dared not meet their father's terrifying gaze.

"I may not like what has happened, but it happened and we must do what is right. Shangó, you must take Oshún to be your third wife."

"But Baba!" protested Shangó "Dada and Yemaya will be furious."

"They'll have to accept things as they are. You two are to be married, and Oshún must be set up in a grand palace worthy of her stature."

How Oshún came to Cuba

During the shameful days of the slave trade, Oshún saw thousands upon thousands of her devotees being taken away from their homes in Africa to faraway lands. Frustrated, the Orisha of rivers was somehow unable to keep this horrible deed from occurring. As she often did when troubled, Oshún sought solace in the maternal arms of her big sister, Queen Yemaya, who told her that there were some mysteries not even the Orisha could decipher.

"Yemaya, you whose oceans touch every land, where are all our children being taken to?"

"They are being taken to many places, see those ships there in the harbor?" The stately queen pointed to two large vessels. "They are going to end up in Cuba, in fact, many of our people will end up in Cuba."

Becoming pensive for a moment, Oshun asked Yemaya, "What is Cuba like?"

"It is very much like here, lush vegetation, tranquil rivers, beautiful beaches, clear blue skies."

"What about the people, Dear Sister, are they like us?"

"No, they are not all black like us. Some are black, some are whi.. some are red, some are brown, and a few are yellow."

Without thinking twice, Oshun said: "I want to go with them! I want to be there to help my children in this their hour of need! But before I go, Yemaya, you who knows so many secrets of the ocean depths, make my hair straighter and my complexion lighter so that all Cubans can see a little of themselves in me!"

With a majestic sweep of her hand Yemaya changed Oshún's hair from extremely curly to long and wavy, and her complexion from dark ebony to golden honey. Shortly after her arrival in Cuba, everyone fell in love with Oshún, the island being dedicated to Oshún by all the elders. All Cubans, no matter what the color of their skins, worship their beloved bella mulata together.

Commentary: This transparently obvious fabrication was concocted to explain why Oshún is depicted as a woman of mixed ancestry. On a deeper level, however, this story demonstrates the overwhelming popularity of Oshún in Cuba.

Yemayá changes Oshún's appearance

task of igniting nearly every male Orisha with ~~herself~~ no longer the girlish spitfire that she had ~~retired~~ to the forest. There she lived a life of deep meditation ~~and~~ simplicity, befriending the vulture as well as the peacock, washing her one dress every night so she could wear it clean the next morning. The fabric yellowed from so many washes, but at this stage of her life Oshún was no longer the vain fashion plate she had been. It was also at this time that her powers became enormously focused, eventually making her an unparalleled force. It was at this time that Orula, head diviner of the gods, came to pay a visit to the somewhat dowdy, yet still striking goddess.

"What brings the greatest diviner of all times to the presence of this plain old woman?" asked Oshún.

The ever-gallant Orula, much older than Oshún, gave the goddess a huge sunflower, her favorite flower. "You are still the most breathtaking beauty of all, My Lady, only now your beauty is framed by your wisdom and simplicity."

"I hope you know, Orula, that I've also become much less patient, what is it that you really want?"

Smiling slightly, Orula says: "At the moment, we are both unattached. Marry me, Oshún, be the guardian of my secrets!"

Oshún accepted and, to celebrate the moment, Orunla ordered that from then on the necklaces and bracelets his devotees wore would be green and yellow instead of green and red, so that all could see the pairing of his green with Oshún's yellow. It is said that of all of Orula's wives, Oshún was his most efficient. Since that time, it has been customary for priests of Orunla to marry priestesses of Oshún.

How Oshún obtained the secret of cowry-shell reading from Obatala

All the Orisha wanted to have the right to divine using cowry shells, but only two knew how; Obatala and Orula. Although Obatala loved his children dearly, he absolutely refused to share with them that gift which God Almighty gave only to him and Orula. Eshu, Lord of Destiny, decided to help Oshún achieve that which no other orisha had achieved, learning the secret of divination. It was when Obatala took a bath at a brook near Oshún's dwelling that Eshu told her to steal Obatala's clothes. The King of the White Cloth couldn't possibly be seen naked, so Oshún hid his clothes and asked Obatala to tell her the secret. Obatala would have refused, even if it meant him never leaving the brook, but the vision of the heavenly goddess totally covered in golden honey so pleased the great god Obatala that he gave in and showed her how to throw the cowry shells. So mad was Orula when he found out, that he swore never to use cowry shells again, using palm nuts instead.

Commentary: This pataki is not too often told in Cuba, but is widely told in Africa. In Cuba, Yemayá is more often singled out as the one who took the secret. In this version, however, it was Oshún who with her beauty mystified Obatala into giving her the power to divine the future, a power she selflessly shared with the rest of her brethren Orisha.

Oshún, Oya and Yemayá set up business as Diviners

After Oshún shared with Yemayá and Oya the secret of how to divine using the shells, they decided that they should become partners forming a joint practice. Oshún proposed that they also bring in Eshu Laroye, Lord of Communications, to handle the advertising. They all agreed to divide each day's take equally in four parts. Soon the firm of Oshún, Yemayá, Oya and Laroye, cowry shell divination experts, flourished. They acquired a comfortable place by the beach, where Laroye would send them client after client. He would stand in a bustling intersection telling everyone about the sisters. In the beginning all was well, the considerable bounty that was collected each day would be fairly divided among the four partners. Soon, however, the three sisters began to have doubts about Laroye, thinking they were paying him too much. At first they began to cut his part a little here and there, until they finally stopped giving him anything. At that point, Laroye stood by the road that led to the beach house, turning all clients away. "Yemayá, Oshún, and Oya do not live here anymore," Eshu Laroye would say. After a few days, the sisters called Laroye up to speak with him.

"Where are the clients?" Oya wanted to know.

"We are starving here!" said Oshún.

"I guess the clients went the same way my part of the profits went," Laroye answered. "I haven't seen any for days!"

Oshún immediately recognized the wrong they had committed and asked Laroye for forgiveness. "Furthermore" the regal beauty stated--"Eshu Laroye's profit will be the first separated, his food will be the first served, his portion of money the first taken aside for him."

The sisters did this and their practice again flourished.

How Oshún made Ogun fall in love with Yemayá

Ogun Onire lived near the river in a hut away from mankind. Tales of how he savagely took women, having intercourse with them and later abandoning them, reached Yemayá, whose curiosity was aroused by the stories. "I want to experience this savage lover," Yemayá said to herself. She went by the river and, sure enough, Onire pounced upon her, making her his and afterwards abandoning her. Yemayá demanded to be satisfied again, but Onire refused. Brokenhearted, Yemayá went to her sister

Oshún's house to cry on her shoulder because, by this time, she had fallen hopelessly in love with the bearded brute. Oshún devised a plan to make Onire fall in love with Yemayá. Pouring her magic honey all over her supple body, the Orisha of sensuality then tied five yellow sheer scarves around her waist and went to meet Onire. Oshún danced her special dance of the five veils for Onire, who pounced upon her, making her his with savage fury.

Enticed by Oshún's magic honey, Onire said, "Let's do it again!"

But Oshún replied, "not here! It will be better in my house."

Onire followed Oshún, but instead of leading him to her own house, she led him to Yemayá's house. In the darkness, Onire thought he was with Oshún. When morning came and Onire saw Yemayá, he realized he was in love with her, marrying her shortly thereafter.

Oshún in Yorubaland

According to pataki being taught in modern-day Yorubaland (Southwestern Nigeria), in Africa, it isn't Yemaya who married Orunla and stole for all others the secrets of divination. It is none other than Oshún! Another African pataki, not known in Cuba, has Oshún tricking Orunla into bringing her to the manifest world by carrying her in his own abdomen! Her place as the Yoruba Aphrodite, however, is just as obvious in Yorubaland as it is in Cuban Santeria. Is she not the only one who with her feminine honey could entice Ogun from his beloved forest? Was she not the first female to master the divination system of Ifa that was so zealously guarded by Orunla?

Oshún was also the devious wife of Shango, the one that caused Oba to sacrifice her ear. Originally the goddess of a single river, Oshún has become THE water goddess, who rules over all watery domains, including the fluid entrails of a fetal environment. By filling a woman's stomach, she can bring forth bodies that accept the spirits of the ancestors so they can be reborn! While in Cuban Santeria she is called *"la mas chiquita "* (the [hierarchically] smallest), Yoruba theologians call her the first female irunmole--the irunmole being a class of being higher than an orisha, akin to an archangel in JudeoChristian belief. The irunmole Oshún represents the cosmic force LOVE as it manifests in the worlds of matter, thoughts, sensations and spirits. She is Olodumare's boundless love personified in the form of a woman.

The following are excerpts from various ORIKI (praise poems) that describe the many facets of Oshún.

Oshun, oyeyeni mo...
Oshún who is full of understanding...

O wa yanrin wayanrin kowo si
Who digs sand and buries money there

Obinrin gbona, okunrin nsa
The woman who seizes the road and causes men to run away

Oshun abura-olu
Oshun the river which the king cannot exhaust
One who does things without being questioned

Ogbadagbada loyan
One who has large robust breasts

Oye ni mo, eni ide kii su
One who has fresh palm leaves, who is never tired of wearing brass

Gbadamufbadamu obinrin ko See gbamu...
The huge, powerful woman who cannot be attacked

Ore yeye o
Most gracious mother

Onikii, amo-awo maro
Onikii, who knows the secret of cults but does not disclose them.

Yeye onikii, obalodo
The gracious mother, the queen of the river.

Otutu nitee
One who has a cool, fresh throne

Iya ti ko leegun, ti ko leje
The mother who has neither bone nor blood

Oshún has not achieved as widespread an appeal in Africa as she has in the New World. In fact, in Yorubaland proper, her worship is mainly concentrated on the town of Oshogbo. There her priests know how to heighten the beneficial properties of minerals found in her waters, and how to communicate with the Orisha through her messengers and symbols. In Oshogbo, it is said that even the *alejo* (uninitiated) can feel Oshún's presence! For example, some strange natural sculptures common around the river, seem to be representations of the goddess! Tall clumps of meadow plants whose white seeds may be picked and strung into necklaces seem to have been planted just for that. Here and there on the flat rocks lie dark brown locust pods whose vanished seeds have left dents large as thumbprints. These pods can be strung into anklets for Oshún's dancers.

There are two different stories of the founding of Oshogbo. They do not make sense in linear time, but Africans are on spiral time, where everything is possible. The first story says that when the ruler of Ipole in Ijesha country died, his sons quarreled over his beauteous gowns. While the vain princes fought for the showy materials, the late king's daughter, Ogidan, said to be built like a brick house and be as strong as an avalanche, took the dead king's beaded crown and wore it, leading an exodus of mostly women in search of a better place to live. Through the forest they went and eventually arrived at a wondrous river, where Ogidan, who was pregnant, went into labor, so she suggested they settle there. Oshún, however, who used the flat stones around the river to die her clothes ochre, was afraid the settlers would disturb her operation. She offered to protect and aid them if they kept on walking a few more miles. After a few miles, Ogidan could go no further. She called all her people together and while they waited outside a hastily constructed shelter, she gave birth to a child who came into the world carrying Oshún's message! *"This is the place!"* said the newborn child. Ogidan named the new prince *"Ataoja,"* which means: *"He Who Is Born With a Fish in His Hands,"* a title still borne by the king of Oshogbo. In the course of time, Ogidan's brothers found out where she was and threatened to bring war upon the new town if she did not send back the crown. Oshún advised her to do so and in exchange gave her a crown of brass, the metal that transmits the force personified by the river, to present to her son as soon as he grew up.

The second story on the founding of Oshogbo says that the Owe of Ilesha, foremost of the Ijesha kings, sent the successful warrior Laro west to found an outpost along a trade route then in dispute among several neighbrs. But when Laro and his men arrived at the river crossing called *Ofatado* (where the bow and arrow rest), Laro said to his followers,

"Let us put aside our weapons of war and death. Here where we will always find fresh water, let us found a town of our own and forget the turmoil of our former existence."

A few days later one of Laro's daughters, while bathing, disappeared beneath the water. This seemed like a bad omen, but as Laro stood grieving on a large rock overlooking the apparently treacherous inlet, his daughter reappeared, splendidly dressed in a saffron gown, her arms laden with brass and gold bangles.Laro hastened to prepare offerings to bestow upon the river goddess in return for her generous kindness to his daughter. When many fish surfaced to accept his gifts, Laro said, about Oshún.

"This is natural. She is as gracious as my daughter said. Surely all will be well for us from now on."

But when one very large fish suddenly swam close to the place where Laro was seated and spit water upon him, Laro caught the water with his hands cupped and drank it, saying,

"Surely this is an exceptional occasion."

Then he reached out and the large fish leaped into this hands, saying,

"From now on you and your successors may call yourselves *Ataoja* (he who stretches forth his hands and grasps a fish). Furthermore, if you promise not to build here upon my mistress Oshún's sacred bank but, rather, farther up upon the knoll, she will protect your town forever."

"In that case," said Ataoja, "I shall call my city Oshogbo (mature Oshún) in honor of her abundant waters. Tell her she need not fear to bury her riches in these sands. We will protect them. Tell her further that I will renew our pact each year by making offerings to you, her messengers, and that one person every four days shall be consecrated to her worship."

"In that case," said the fish, "her generosity shall not fail to make your town, her special town, prosper. Don't forget cornmeal and honey are our favorite dishes." And with that he leaped out of the Ataoja's hands and back into the river.

Every year the Ataoja, on behalf of his people, renews the original agreement. But it is a young girl, the sacred Arugba, who really embodies the spirit of the treaty. Alone with four priests the girl, in a deep trance, goes to a secret spot to meet Oshún in person! It is said that the Arugba goes into trance at the very spot where Ogidan had her baby. To the sound of ancient incantations, she also walks softly so the good earth Oshún has blessed will not be hurt, she also walks softly so that Oshún is not startled. Two bitter kola nuts inside her mouth remind her never to reveal the wonders she has been priviledged to experience. Such is the story of Oshogbo, the town where Oshún's worship was born.

Oshún, Godess of Sensuality

2

ATTRIBUTES

Necklaces

Oshún's "generic" necklace is made by alternating five bright yellow beads with five amber-colored ones until desired length is reached. Each of her paths, however, has a particular pattern. Here are some of them.

Oshún Ibu Kolé: 15 honey-colored beads followed by one green, five red, and one black, faceted, jet bead (azabache), until desired length is reached.

Oshún Ibu Anya: 15 honey-colored beads followed by five red, five deep-yellow beads, one red, one amber, one red, until desired length is reached.

Oshún Ibu Akuaro: 15 honey-colored, followed by five red, plus a few mother-of-pearl beads interspersed here and there.

Oshún Olo Lodi: 15 honey-colored beads, five yellow, five green, one amber, until desired length is reached.

Oshún Yummu: 15 honey-colored beads, five yellow, and lots of, other-of-pearl and amber beads interspersed here and there.

Emblematic colors, number, elements, dominion, and Catholic disguise:

Oshún's emblematic color is yellow, particularly yellow gingham. Her number is 5. She rules over rivers and gold. Brass and copper are also associated with her. Oshún is the goddess of love and also of childbirth. She has dominion over the abdominal area. Oshún protects women during childbirth and prostitutes.

Initiation names for priests of Oshún:

Oshún Beleyé
Oshún Told
Oshún Lokiki
Oshún Oñiosun
Oshún Were
Oshún Blé
Oshún Ilari
Oshún Ati Elewa
Oshún Ladé
Oshún Guñe
Oshún Kada
Oshún Leti
Oshún Teki
Oshún Nike
Oshún Funké
Oshún Gayedé
Oshún Dere
Oshún Gumi
Oshún Kere
Oshún Arike
Oshún Lai
Oshún Fumike
Oshún Tinibú
Oshún Titiwa

Oshún Bi
Oshún Soino
Oshún Sele
Oshún Soino
Oshún Sele
Oshún Di
Oshún Oreladi
Oshún Iñare
Oshún Rai
Oshún Korá
Oshún Don
Oshún Tuyu
Oshún Loya
Oshún Fumi Loro
Oshún Yari
Oshún Elere
Oshún Amoremi
Oshún Kantomi
Oshún Titilai
Ibu Akuara
Odoró
Tino Tino
Ayini

Shrine (igbodu) - How initiates honor Oshún

Oshún's mysteries are usually kept inside a beautifully decorated yellow soup tureen. These are five river stones, a full hand of cowry shells (about 18), five brass bangles, two oars, five brass nails, a sun, a five-pointed star, and a half-moon. Sometimes a brass crown tops her tureen. Brass or peacock-feather fans, corals, shells, and dried starfish are used as decorations.

Shrine (ojubo alejo) - How non-initiates may honor Oshún

Non-Initiates can honor Oshún by setting up an altar featuring mermaids, combs, mirrors, and photographs of rivers. This altar can be decorated with peacock feathers, golden chains, sunflowers, yellow roses etc.

Offerings (adimu):

Oshún loves honey, oranges, cinnamon, pastries, custards, and colognes.

Blood offerings (ebó):

She loves hens, guinea fowl, pidgeons, ducks, quails, peacocks, canaries, alligators, and castrated goats.

Characteristics of Oshún (and of her devotees):

Oshún is sensual and expressive, yet she is deceptively lighthearted and can be callous. She is said to fan herself and laugh at the funerals of those who have betrayed her. She is strict in demanding that promises made to her be kept, and expects to receive proper and fair payment for any service she provides. She is the most beautiful female and the most gracious, a natural dancer whose moves can excite the coldest male to a heated frenzy. In her crone aspect she is accompanied by vultures and is a supremely gifted sorceress. Oshún's children are beautiful women and men who know how to use their looks to get ahead in life. They are very charming, but can be somewhat superficial and may hold grudges.

Oshún's Catholic disguise is Our Lady of Charity from the township of Cobre, in Cuba, who was declared the Catholic patron saint of Cuba in 1916 by Pope Benedict XV. Her feast day is September 8, her salutation, *Yalodde!*

Herbs and plants:
Cinnamon, vetiver, witch hazel, sunflower, anise, indigo, sweet potato, pumpkin, spinach, mint, rose.

Our Lady of Charity (La Caridad del Cobre)

Oshún Ibu Kolé
The crone aspect of Oshún

ROADS OF OSHÚN:

Oshún Yeyé Moró, also called Oshún Yeyé Kari and Oshún Panchagara: "La Santa Puta." the Holy Whore, the sensuous, coquettish, party-loving avatar of the goddess, protector of prostitutes.

Oshún Kayode: Similar to Oshún Yeyé Moró, but also known for her generous, selfless nature.

Oshún Miwá: Another seductress avatar of the goddess.

Oshún Aña or Ayan: Protects drummers.

Oshún Yummu, Oshún Bunmi, Oshún Gumi: In these guises Oshún is of severe character and serious nature. These avatars are identified with fisher folk and those who manufacture fishing nets. Oshún Yummu is very old and hard of hearing, she manufactures porcelain vases and cups. Yummu is very wealthy and very severe. She had relations with Ogun. Oshún Bunmi protects those who work with the dead, such as spirit mediums. She rocks herself on a rocking chair at the bottom of the river.

Oshún Sakesé is the most serious of all.

Oshún Akuará lives in brackish waters, where the river meets the ocean. She likes to dance and has a pleasant disposition. In this aspect, Oshún enjoys healing the sick and helping children "born to die" (abiku) survive infancy. Oshún Akuará will not work black magic. She loves to eat quail. Oshún Akuará is depicted as a very tall, stately beauty who enjoys spending money.

Oshún Fumiké is the one that helps women during childbirth, she works closely with Obatala and is protector of children.

Oshún Olo Lodi lives at the bottom of the river, she is a mermaid who can't hear and loves to spend her time knitting. To call her, one has to ring a silver bell loudly. In this avatar, Oshún does not dance.

Oshún Funké: Wisdom personified, protects teachers.

Oshún Edé: An elegant lady, lover of good music.

Oshún Niwé lives in the forest.

Oshún Ibu Kolé: The crone aspect of the goddess, her mysteries are not kept in a soup tureen, but in a gourd adorned with four vulture feathers hung from a high place. In this avatar Oshún is a solitary sorceress that lives with vultures.

Oshún Awé: Protects spirit mediums.

In Arará religion Oshún is called Afradi, in Vodou she is called Erzulie, in Palo she is Mama Shola Wanga.

OSHÚN IN BRAZIL:

In Brazil Oshún is known as "Oxum." She is greeted with the salutation, "Ore-ie-ie-o!" She carries a round, silver fan. Her Catholic disguise is as Our Lady of Candlemas in most parts of Brazil, but in Recife she is Our Lady of Mount Carmel and in Rio Saint Catherine and the Immaculate Conception. Her feast day is either September 8th or July 16th.

Oxum sygill
(Ponto Riscado)

3

OSHÚN AND SANTERÍA'S "CELESTIAL COURT"

Santería is really a fusion of separate Yoruba denominations that, because of the exigencies of the new milieu into which the practitioners of each denomination were forced to face in the New World, became a single religion. In Africa, worshippers of Oshún formed a distinct denomination - an "egbe." In Yoruba culture, all the other Orisha, with some exceptions such as Ogun and Eshu, were worshipped exclusively by their respective egbes, the different egbes having little or nothing to do with each other. In Cuba and other New World places, enslaved Yoruba found themselves in danger of losing their culture, as they did in non-Catholic colonies. Hiding under the quasi-pagan beliefs of popular Catholicism, the Yoruba found it expedient to merge their egbes into a synthesis that came to be known as "Santería."

In Santería, Oshún presents something of a paradox. Although she is called *"la mas chica"* (the smallest) in reference to her hierarchical status, she is nevertheless acknowledged as God Almighty's favorite daughter and is without a doubt Santería's most popular orisha! Even white society matrons who would never think of themselves as practicing Santería join the processions that salute the Virgin of Cobre by vigorously waving yellow scarves high above their heads, an African-style salute to Oshún. Because of her vitality, her apparent humanity, her love of life, and her sentimental nature, Oshún presents an irresistible icon to the Cuban people.

Her mixed-race appearance, her unabashed sponsorship of "Cuban-ness," and her willingness to sacrifice for her children make Oshún the orisha for Cubans everywhere. The same qualities that have endeared Cuban music, Cuban films, and Cuban tourism to millions also endear Oshún to many non-Cubans. Of all the Orisha, Oshún has suffered the greatest transformation from her Yoruba origin to her present Cuban status. Her position in Santeria's celestial court is paradoxical; she is the one with less rank, but the most beloved by popular acclaim!

4

Oriki Oshún;
Orin Oshún

PRAYERS AND SONGS TO OSHÚN

*Initiates to the mysteries of Oshún may reinforce their
works with the goddess by reciting these ancient
Yoruba/Lukumi chants and praise poems to Oshún.*

Yoruba is a tonal language. Intonation can make two words that are
spelled the same have dramatically different meanings. Modern Yoruba
has developed a series of punctuation marks that indicate tone and meaning.
When people who spoke what we now call Yoruba first arrived in Cuba,
they had no written language, they therefore used the Spanish alphabet to
write their language, which was called "Lukumi." Thus, abebe (crocodile)
and abebe (fan) are spelled identically in Lukumi. Since tone was gradually
lost in Cuba, only context and tradition remained to indicate what was
meant. The translation I grew up with of the following song to Oshún
makes more sense to us in Cuba than the translation John Mason
provides, since we in Cuba are acquainted with the aspect of Oshún that
presents herself bearing a fan, fanning herself. We think of the crocodile
more as an animal associated with Olokun. I am providing both translations
here since, in Santeria, multiple realities are the norm rather than the
exception.

ORIN ORISA 1
(Lukumi chant)

Beroni abebe Oshún
Beroni abebe eleda
Beroni abebe Oshún
Beroni abebe leda
Iya Yummu bakaraleda
Beroni abebe Oshún

Grand Lady, owner of the fan, Oshún.
Grand Lady, owner of the fan, supreme being.
Grand Lady, owner of the fan, Oshún.
Grand Lady, owner of the fan, supreme being.
Pregnant Mother, goddess.
Grand Lady, owner of the fan, Oshún.

ORIN ORISA 1
(John Mason's version)

Be oni abebe Osun
Be oni abebe eye da
Be oni abebe Osun
Be oni abebe eye da
Iya yunnu bara laare gba
Be oni abebe Osun.

Beg the crocodile, the petitioner of Osun.
Beg the crocodile, the petitioner suitable by nature.
Beg the crocodile, the petitioner of Osun.
Beg the crocodile, the petitioner suitable by nature.
Mothers pregnant with stomachs beg to receive a favorable verdict.
Beg the crocodile, the petitioner of Osun.

ORIKI OXUM
(Brazil)

My mother Oxum,
Queen of lakes and streams.
My mother Oxum,
hear our prayers!
Near the waterfall
there is a little cave,
near the waterfall,
there is a little golden bench;
near the waterfall,
my mother Oxum
often comes to rest.

ORIKI OSHÚN
(Cuba)

Oshún kerekete mi owo,
Omi dara omi dara omi dara.
Oshún kerekete mi owo
Omi dara omi dara omi dara

Little Oshún, grant me money
Beautiful water, beautiful water, beautiful water
Little Oshún, grant me money
Beautiful water, beautiful water, beautiful water

ORIKI OSHÚN

(Yoruba, translated by Ulli Beier)

Brass and parrot feathers
on a velvet skin.
White cowrie shells
on black buttocks.
Her eyes sparkle in the forest
she is the wisdom of the river.
Where the doctor failed
she cures with fresh water,
Where medicine is impotent
she cures with cool water.
She cures the child
and does not charge the father.
She feeds the barren woman with honey
and her dry body swells up
like a juicy palm fruit.
Oh how sweet
is the touch of a child's hand! [2]

ORIN OSHÚN

Barewa lele
Umale
Arele umawo
Alabe Oshún
Oshún mirere-o.

The beautiful one emerges The spirit-god One of the family
reincarnated Honor to Oshún's knife My good Oshún.

5

DESPOJOS / CLEANSINGS & SPELLS

OSHÚN'S CLEANSING BATH

Of all the cleansings I have recommended in my thirty-eight years as an orisha priest, I can unequivocally state that this is the one that has been most consistently successful. While some people who have done it have told me that this cleansing has literally changed their lives, no one has ever reported any negative effects from it; actually, the most common remark I've heard is *"I feel so much better after having taken the Oshún baths!"* It is important that the instructions be followed to the letter.

INGREDIENTS

FIVE YELLOW ROSES, PETALS ONLY
FIVE CINNAMON STICKS
FIVE DIFFERENT COLOGNES (FIVE DROPS FROM EACH)
FIVE DROPS OF HONEY
FIVE DROPS OF FLORIDA WATER

1. On a Tuesday evening, mix all ingredients on a pail of water.

2. Place pail by a window where the first light of Wednesday morning will hit it.

3. After the Sun's rays have touched the water with all of the ingredients, you are ready to add to your bath water.

4. Light a yellow candle and settle into your bath, relaxing for at least twenty minutes, asking Oshún to grant your wishes.

5. Do this every Wednesday for five weeks in a row.

You'll be amazed at the results. This bath not only makes the person taking it more attractive all-around, it also brings good fortune and good health!

A much simpler Oshún bath for attracting lovers *involves bathing with five whole oranges floating in your bathwater. Play with them, pass them all over your body as you ask Oshún for a mate.*

Oshún bath for attracting prosperity:
An Oshún bath for prosperity contains five bunches of parsley, a glass of milk, and five drops of honey. You can use the water from the bath (before you bathe in it) as a floor wash also.

Oshún bath for attracting good luck:
Mix two teaspoons of cinnamon, 3 ounces of Three Kings incense, and one ounce of Amber incense, burn on q uick-burning charcoal in the name of Oshún throughout your house for good luck.

GAIN THE LOVE OF "THAT CERTAIN" PERSON

Write his name on a parchment and prepare an Oshún lamp as follows: Take a pumpkin or squash that is as round as possible. Cut the top 1/3 of it and hollow out. When you have a bowl-like squash in your hands, add cinnamon oil, olive oil, five drops of honey, five pennies, Oshún oil, and golden glitter to it. Light a floating wick on it and put the name of person neatly folded under the lamp. He will be yours before the lamp is consumed.

DREAM OF YOUR FUTURE HUSBAND

Mix the following ingredients into your bathwater:

5 YELLOW ROSES (PETALS ONLY)
5 WHOLE ORANGES
5 WHOLE CANTALOUPES
5 CINNAMON STICKS

Also place 1 medium-sized hand mirror in the tub

• After bathing, gather all solids from the bathtub and place them in a bag.

• Place the mirror under your bed.

• Take bag to the river drop it in the water along with 5 pennies, saying:

"Mother Oshún, let me my future husband at five in the morning see."

(continued)

• *Go straight home and go to bed.*

• *Wake up at five in the morning, by the light of a candle you had lit before you went to bed, look at the mirror. You'll see the face of your future husband.*

OSHÚN'S ATTRACTION ESSENCE

In her wonderful tome *Yemaya y Ochun,* the great Cuban ethnographer Lydia Cabrera gave the recipe for what she calls the "Mother Formula" or most potent attraction essence ever designed.

Place the following ingredients into a 1 gallon jug (preferably on a Good Saturday of Easter week):

CINNAMON EXTRACT	BENZOIN
ANISE EXTRACT	HOLY WATER
1 TEASPOON OF LEMON JUICE	GROUND YAM
APPLE BLOSSOM EXTRACT	SANDALWOOD
ROSEMARY	A SLUG [A SNAIL CAN BE SUBSTITUTED]

THREE DIFFERENT KINDS OF MERCURY [3]

SOME MOONSHINE LIQUOR AND SOME RUM

PETALS FROM THE FOLLOWING FOUR FLOWERS:
FORGET-ME-NOTS, PANSIES, ROSES, AND LILLIES

THE FOLLOWING HERBS:
RUE, MIMOSA, YAMAO, PARAMI, AMANSA GUAPO,
AND DUERMETE PUTA [4]

Add HIGH JOHN THE CONQUEROR ROOT *and* THREE DROPS OF YOUR URINE TO THE MIX, *plus* THREE DROPS OF URINE FROM A BITCH IN HEAT

Say the "PRAYER OF THE LONELY SOUL" *three times, and leave gallon by Eleggua Laye's altar for three days. Eleggua Laye opens the door to all of the Orishas.*

This perfume is to be used on the hands, face, and handkerchief of person who will now be irresistible"[5]

Another one of Cabrera's informants, Nina, the self-described *"Santera to fine white ladies"* offered the following recipe for an **Attraction Powder:**

> *Expensive after-shower body powder mixed with Apple Blossom extract and ground Basil.* [6]

Although much less complicated when compared to the *"Mother Formula,"* Nina swore by her powder.

OSHÚN'S FAVORITE DISH

Whenever you want to gain Oshún's favor, simply prepare her favorite dish, Ochinchin, which is made of cleaned, de-veined shrimp, eggs, and boiled collard greens. Use five shrimp, five beaten eggs, and about a cup of boiled greens, mix well and fry as an omelette, give to Oshún by the river along with five pennies.

---

[1] Ulli Beier, Yoruba Poetry, Cambridge: Cambridge University Press, 1970. p. 33.

[2] Ibid.

[3] Because of the dangers associated with the use of mercury, either use extremely little or dispense with this ingredient.

[4] I don't know the English names of these, but most well-stocked botanicas will carry them.

[5] Lydia Cabrera, Yemaya y Ochun (Madrid: C.R., 1974), p. 313.

[6] Ibid.

BABALÚ AYÉ

SANTERÍA AND THE LORD OF PESTILENCE

BY BABA RAUL CANIZARES
& ABURO ERIC LERNER

BABALU GIVES HIS DEVOTEES MEANS TO SURVIVE. ULLI BEIER, A SEASONED SCHOLAR AND POET OF YORUBA CULTURE, ELABORATES ON THIS POINT:

"SAKPATA [BABALU] IS THE GOD OF SUFFERING. HE TEACHES HIS WORSHIPPERS TO COPE WITH MISFORTUNES (PARTICULARLY DISEASE). IF SAKPATA STRIKES A MAN WITH SMALLPOX, IT IS BECAUSE HE WANTS TO ESTABLISH A VERY CLOSE RELATIONSHIP WITH THAT PERSON. ONLY THE MAN WHO IS NOT MATURE ENOUGH OR STRONG ENOUGH WILL DIE OF THE DISEASE. FOR THE WORTHY PERSON IT IS LIKE AN INITIATION: A DEATH AND RESURRECTION INTO A MATURER, RICHER LIFE."

ORIGINAL PUBLICATIONS
1 (888) OCCULT-1

ORIGINAL PUBLICATIONS

Send **$2.00** for our complete catalog of over 600 titles. Santeria, Yoruba, Voodoo, Candle Burning, Herbs, Oils, Spells, Dreams, Kabbalah, Self Help, Prayer, Astrology, Tarot, and Spanish Language. ☐

- ☐ THE PSALM WORKBOOK; Robert Laremy $7.95
- ☐ PAPA JIM'S HERBAL MAGIC WORKBOOK; Papa Jim $6.95
- ☐ POWERFUL POTIONS OF SANTERIA; Carlos Montenegro $6.95
- ☐ DREAM YOUR LUCKY LOTTERY NUMBER; Raul Canizares $5.95
- ☐ NEW REVISED MASTER BOOK OF CANDLEBURNING $5.95
- ☐ HELPING YOURSELF WITH SELECTED PRAYERS $4.95
- ☐ SPIRITUAL CLEANSING: A Handbook of Psychic Protection; Mickaharic $6.95
- ☐ NEW REV. 6&7 BKS. OF MOSES; Wippler $9.95
- ☐ HELPING YOURSELF WITH WHITE MAGIC; Pelton $5.95
- ☐ THE MAGIC CANDLE; Charmaine Dey $4.95
- ☐ VOODOO & HOODOO; by Jim Haskins - $12.95
- ☐ VOODOO CHARMS & TALISMANS; Robert Pelton $8.95
- ☐ MYSTERY OF LONG LOST 8, 9, 10 BOOKS OF MOSES - Gamache $5.95
- ☐ PROTECTION CHARMS & SPELLS by Jade-$5.95
- ☐ MONEY MAGIC by Jade - $5.95
- ☐ LOVE CHARMS AND SPELLS; Jade $5.95
- ☐ SANTERIA FORMULARY & SPELLBOOK; Montenegro $14.95
- ☐ SANTERIA; AFRICAN MAGIC IN LATIN AMERICA; Wippler $10.95
- ☐ SANTERIA EXPERIENCE; Wippler $8.95
- ☐ RITUALS & SPELLS OF SANTERIA; Wippler $7.95
- ☐ OLODUMARE; God in Yoruba Belief, Idowu $14.95
- ☐ POWERS OF THE ORISHAS; Wippler $8.95
- ☐ MAGICAL HERBAL BATHS OF SANTERIA - Montenegro - $5.95
- ☐ READING YOUR FUTURE IN THE CARDS; Eden - $5.95
- ☐ AGANJU; Sant. & the Orisha of the Volcano & Wilderness - Canizares $4.95
- ☐ SHANGO; Santeria and the Orisha of Thunder; Canizares $4.95
- ☐ ESHU- ELEGGUA;Santeria & Orisha of the Crossroads; Canizares $4.95
- ☐ OCHOSI: Ifa & the Spirit of the Tracker; Fatunmbi $4.95
- ☐ OBATALA: Santeria & the White Robed King of Orisha; Canizares $4.95
- ☐ BABALU AYE; Santeria and the Lord of Pestilence; Canizares $4.95
- ☐ OSHUN: Santeria Orisha of Love, Rivers & Sensuality; Canizares $4.95
- ☐ OYA: Ifa and the Spirit of the Wind; Fatunmbi $4.95
- ☐ IBEYI: Children of Miraculous Birth; Stuart Myers $5.00

NAME _____ TELEPHONE _____

ADDRESS _____

CITY _____ STATE _____ ZIP _____

TO ORDER BY MASTERCARD, VISA OR AMERICAN EXPRESS
CALL TOLL FREE (888) 622-8581 -OR- (516) 454-6809.

TO ORDER BY MAIL: CHECK THE BOXES NEXT TO YOUR SELECTIONS. ADD THE TOTAL. SHIPPING COSTS ARE $3.50 FOR THE FIRST BOOK PLUS 75 CENTS FOR EACH ADDITIONAL BOOK. NEW YORK STATE RESIDENTS PLEASE ADD 8.25% SALES TAX. ALL ORDERS SHIP IN 14 DAYS. SORRY, NO C.O.D.'S. **SEND ORDERS TO THE ADDRESS BELOW.**

OSHUN

ORIGINAL PUBLICATIONS • P.O. BOX 236, OLD BETHPAGE. NY 11804-0236